4. Shake paint (and textile medium) thoroughly before using. Pour a small puddle of paint onto your palette. If you are using acrylic paint and textile medium, pour an equal amount of textile medium next to the paint puddle. Mix the textile medium into the paint thoroughly. If you are mixing colors, be sure to mix them thoroughly too. Have a disposable cup or bowl of water and some paper towels handy to rinse and wipe your brush when necessary.

5. Choose soft, synthetic brushes for painting. Use a flat brush for filling in the larger areas of the design and a small round brush for filling in smaller areas. A thin liner brush will be invaluable for outlining and detailing. Matching size of brush to the size of the area you wish to paint, dip brush into paint being careful not to get too much paint on brush. You don't want to get paint into the metal part of the paintbrush. Wipe any excess paint onto your palette and begin painting your design. Evenly apply a thin, solid coat of paint to each area. Several thin coats of paint may be required to get adequate coverage. Be sure to allow one color to dry before using another color or adding the next coat. It is a good idea to stop and clean your brush occasionally while painting; however, don't leave your paintbrushes standing in water.

6. If paint splatters on your garment, use a paring knife to gently scrape off paint before it dries; remove stain with non-acetone nail polish remover. If this doesn't work, try to gently wash it out with soap and water while the paint is still wet; try not to get the whole garment wet. Even if you can't get the spot out, you can cover it with a button, a bow, a lace motif, or a dimensional fabric paint design.

7. Allow design to dry completely before redrawing any lost outlines or detail lines with a permanent felt-tip pen.

8. ⬚ ⬚ ⬚ ⬚ ⬚ ⬚ dium ⬚ ⬚ one ⬚ ⬚ g, remove freezer paper and plastic-wrapped cardboard or T-shirt form and follow manufacturer's instructions to heat-set painted design.

9. We decorated and personalized some of our garments by adding buttons, bows, ribbons, jewel stones, lace trims, lace motifs, and dimensional squeeze-bottle fabric paint. You can sew or glue the trims to garments and use dimensional paint or glue to adhere jewels. Dimensional squeeze-bottle fabric paints are a bit different than other fabric paints. Read Tips For Using Dimensional Squeeze-Bottle Fabric Paints before applying these paints to your garment.

10. Allow paint to dry at least 72 hours before washing. To launder, turn garment inside out; machine wash on gentle cycle, following paint and/or glue manufacturer's instructions for water temperature. Hang to dry.

TIPS FOR USING DIMENSIONAL SQUEEZE-BOTTLE FABRIC PAINTS

1. Turn the bottle upside down and let paint fill the tip to keep paint flowing smoothly.
2. Clean the tip often with a paper towel.
3. If the tip becomes clogged, insert a straight pin into the opening or remove the tip and clean with warm water.
4. If a mistake is made, use a paring knife to gently scrape off paint before it dries; remove stain with non-acetone nail polish remover or soap and water. Or, camouflage the mistake by incorporating it into the design.
5. Keep painted garment lying flat at least 24 hours to allow the paint to sufficiently set before handling.

We have made every effort to ensure that these instructions are accurate and complete. We cannot, however, be responsible for human error, typographical mistakes, or variations in individual work.

OUR PRECIOUS PALETTE

Part of the appeal
of the Precious Moments
children is their unique colors.
Here we've given you the color palette
that we used for our painted garments.

Flesh - 1

Hair - 2 or 3

Clothing - 2, 3, 4, 5, 6, 7, 8, 9, 10, 11,
and white

Shoes - 2, 4, 5, 7, 8, 11, 12, and white

Flowers, umbrellas, birds, animals,
and other details in your design
may be painted any
of the colors.

Love Is Patient

I'm A Possibility

Jesus Loves Me

The Lord Is My Shepherd

We Saw A Star

Jesus Is The Answer

You Are Always In My Heart

His Eye Is On The Sparrow

Easter's On Its Way

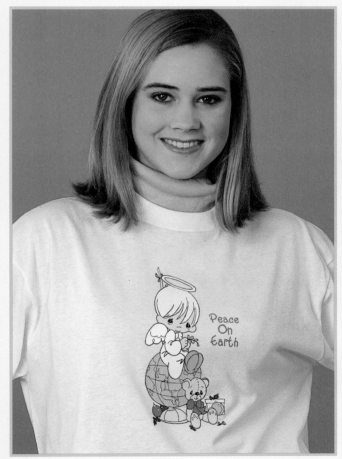

Peace
On
Earth

God Is Love, Dear Valentine

Rejoice

9

Make A Joyful Noise

Make A Joyful Noise

Make A Joyful Noise

Test Transfer

Jesus Loves Me

Jesus Loves Me

11

Jesus Loves Me

Love One Another

Love One Another

12

Love One Another

Test Transfer

Jesus Is The Light

Jesus Is The Light

Jesus Is The Light

God Loveth A Cheerful Giver

God Loveth A Cheerful Giver

Love Is Kind

Love Is Kind

15

He Leadeth Me

16

He Leadeth Me

Test Transfer

Jesus Is The Answer

Jesus Is The Answer

17

Jesus Is The Answer

I Love to Tell the Story

Test Transfer

I Love To Tell The Story

I Love To Tell The Story

You Can't Run Away From God

You Can't Run
Away From God

Not intended for resale.

© 1996, PMI

To God Be The Glory

To God Be The Glory

To God Be The Glory

Jesus Is The Only Way

Jesus Is The Only Way

God Is Love

God Is Love

God Is Love

Onward Christian Soldiers

Onward Christian Soldiers

24

Onward Christian Soldiers

Test Transfer

© 1996, PMI

Not intended for resale.

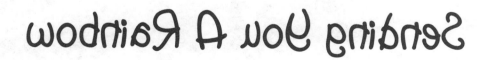
Sending You A Rainbow

25

Sending You A Rainbow

Test Transfer

I Will Make You Fishers Of Men

26

I Will Make You Fishers Of Men

Test Transfer

Dreams Really Do
Come True

Dreams Really Do Come True

Dreams Really Do
Come True

Test Transfer

May Only Good Things Come Your Way

May Only Good Things
Come Your Way

His Eye Is On The Sparrow

His Eye Is On The Sparrow

29

His Eye Is On The Sparrow

Test Transfer

You Are Always In My Heart

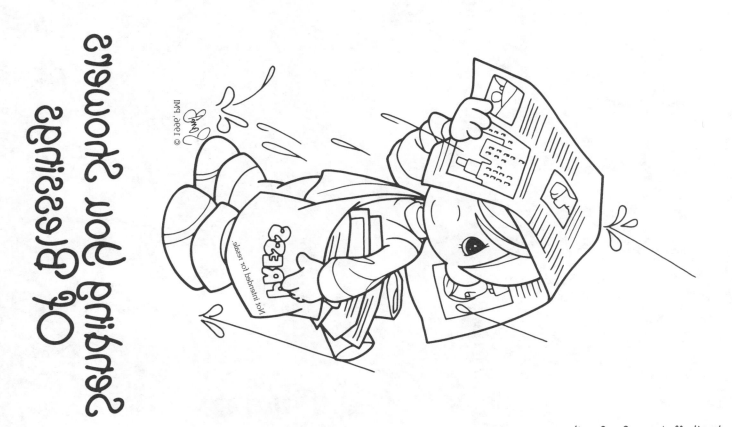

Sending You Showers Of Blessings

You Are Always In My Heart

Sending You Showers Of Blessings

There Shall Be Showers
Of Blessings

There Shall Be Showers Of Blessings

31

There Shall Be Showers
Of Blessings

Test Transfer

I Believe In Miracles

32

I Believe In Miracles

Test Transfer

High Hopes

High Hopes

High Hopes

Thank You For Coming To My Ade

Friendship Grows
When You Plant A Seed

Friendship Grows
When You Plant A Seed

Good Friends Are Forever

Good friends Are forever

Test Transfer

A Friend Is
Someone Who Cares

A Friend Is Someone Who Cares

A Friend Is
Someone Who Cares

Test Transfer

I'm So Glad That God Blessed Me With A Friend Like You

I'm So Glad That God Blessed Me With A Friend Like You

39

I'm So Glad That God
Blessed Me With A
Friend Like You

Test Transfer

His Love Will Shine On You

You Are My Number One

His Love Will Shine On You

You Are My Number One

40

His Love Will
Shine On You

You Are My
Number One

Test Transfer

Cheers To The
Leader

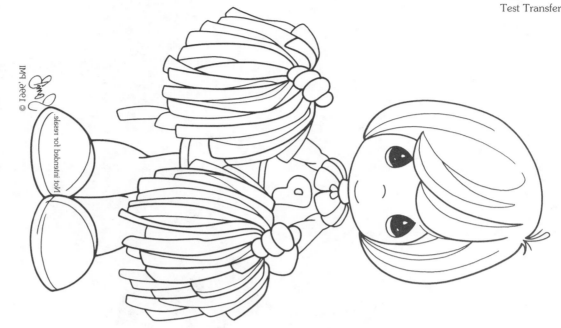

God Bless You
for Touching My Life

Cheers To The Leader

God Bless You For Touching My Life

Test Transfer

Eggspecially for You

Friendship Hits The Spot

42

Eggspecially For You

Friendship Hits The Spot

© 1996, PMI

Test Transfer

44

45

You Have Touched So
Many Hearts

You Have Touched So Many Hearts

You Have Touched So
Many Hearts

Sending You My Love

Sending You My Love

Good News Is So Uplifting

Good News Is So Uplifting

Test Transfer

Let Love Reign

Let Love Reign

Let Love Reign

Love Is Sharing

Love Is Sharing

Love Is Kind

Love Is Kind

Love Is Kind

Love Is Kind

Test Transfer

Hug One Another

Hug One Another

Hug One Another

But Love Goes On Forever

© 1996, PMI

Not intended for resale.

But Love Goes On Forever

But Love Goes On Forever

But Love Goes On Forever

Test Transfer

God Bless Our Home

God Bless Our Home

This Is The Day
Which The Lord Hath Made

Not intended for resale.

© 1996, PM

This Is The Day Which The Lord Hath Made

This Is The Day
Which The Lord Hath Made

Test Transfer

The Lord Bless You
And Keep You

The Lord Bless You And Keep You

The Lord Bless You
And Keep You

Test Transfer

Sharing Our Joy Together

57

Sharing Our Joy Together

Test Transfer

Wishing You Roads Of Happiness

Bless You Two

Wishing You Roads Of Happiness

Bless You Two

58

Wishing You Roads Of Happiness

Bless You Two

Test Transfer

Bon Voyage

Bon Voyage

Precious Memories

Precious Memories

Precious Memories

Test Transfer

To A Very Special Sister

© 1996, PMI

To A Very Special Sister

To A Very Special Sister

Test Transfer

To A Very
Special Mom

Mommy,
I Love You

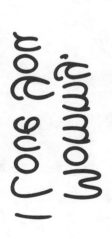

To A Very Special Mom

Mommy, I Love You

62

To A Very
Special Mom

Mommy,
I Love You

Happy Birthday Dad

To A Special Dad

Happy Birthday Poppy

To A Special Dad

63

Happy Birthday
Poppy

To A Special Dad

Test Transfer

May Your Every
Wish Come True

© 1996, PMI

May Your Birthday
Be A Blessing

© 1996, PMI

May Your Every Wish Come True

May Your Birthday Be A Blessing

64

© 1996, PMI

The Joy Of The Lord
Is My Strength

The Joy Of The Lord Is My Strength

The Joy Of The Lord
Is My Strength

Test Transfer

Not intended for resale.
© 1996, PMI

Not intended for resale
© 1996, PMI

67

Test Transfer

Test Transfer

Baby

Not intended for resale.

© 1996, PMI

Jesus Loves me

Not intended for resale.

© 1996, PMI

Jesus Loves Me

Test Transfer

Baby's First Step

Baby's First Step

Baby's First Step

© 1996, PMI

Test Transfer

Heaven
Bless
You

Heaven Bless You

Heaven
Bless
You

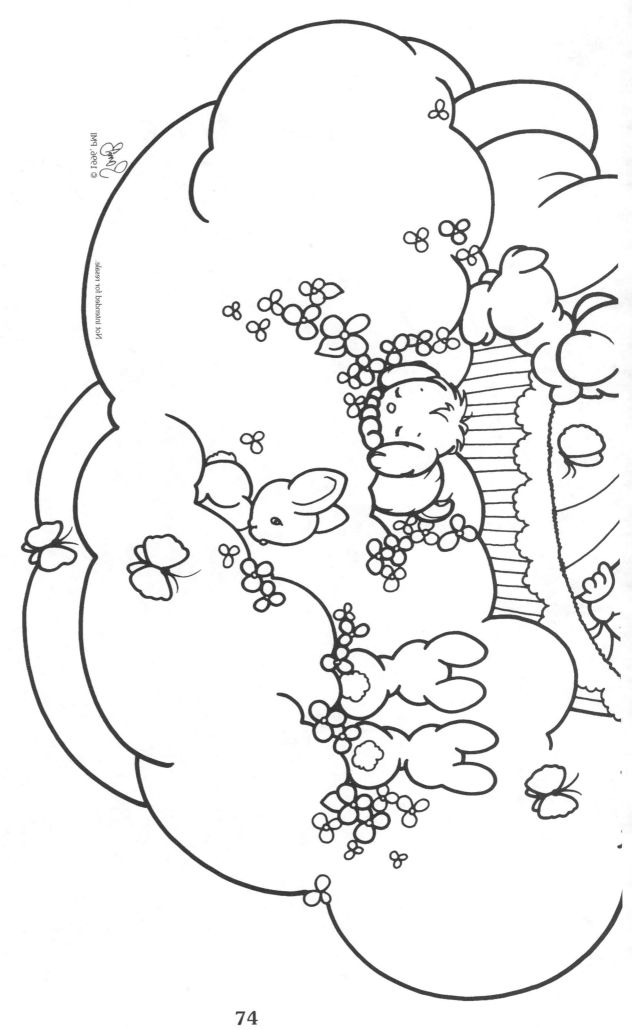

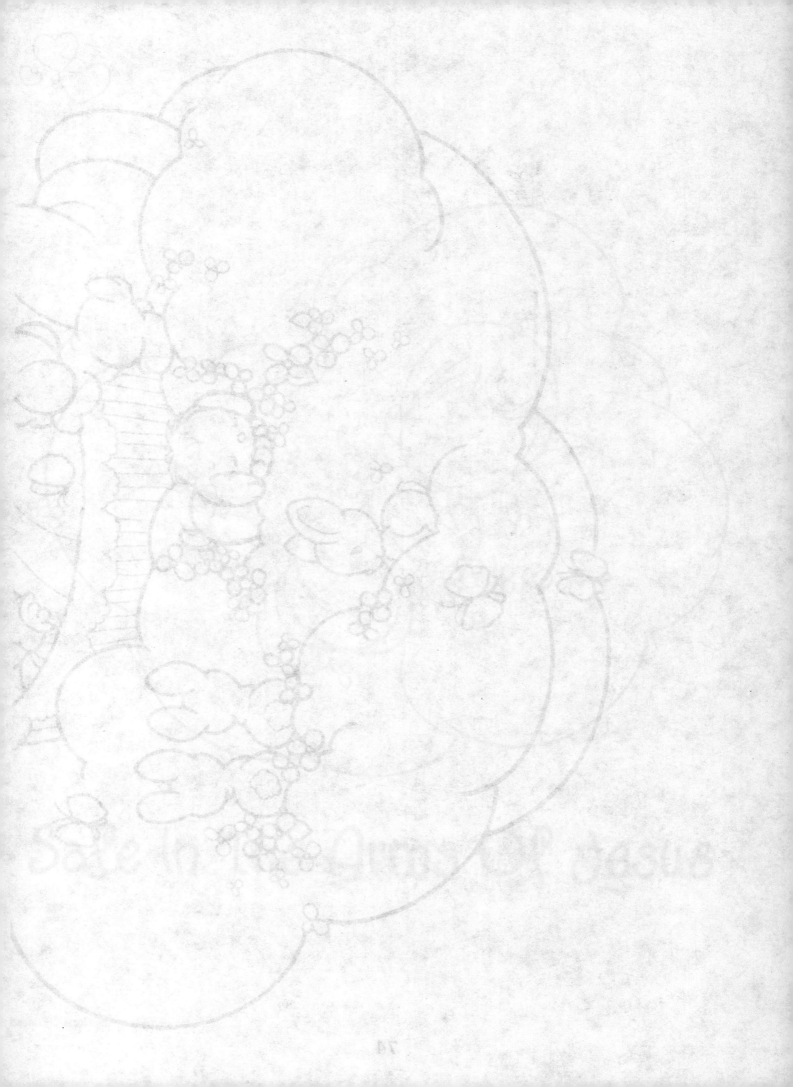

Safe In The Arms Of Jesus

Safe In The Arms Of Jesus

Safe In The Arms Of Jesus

Lord Keep Me On My Toes

© 1996, PMI

Lord Keep Me On My Toes

Lord
Keep Me
On My
Toes

Lord, Turn My Life Around

Lord, Turn My Life Around

The Lord Turned My Life Around

The Lord
Turned
My Life
Around

Test Transfer

I'm A Possibility

I'm A Possibility

79

I'm A Possibility

May Your Life Be Blessed With Touchdowns

May Your Life Be Blessed
With Touchdowns

Test Transfer

Pretty As A Princess

Pretty As A Princess

Pretty As A Princess

Hallelujah Country

Hallelujah Country

Hallelujah Country

Test Transfer

Make The Grade
Lord Help Me

Are Here Again
Happy Days

Lord Help Me Make The Grade

Happy Days Are Here Again

85

Put On A Happy Face

Put On A Happy Face

Happiness Divine

© 1996, PMI

Not intended for resale.

Happiness Divine

87

Happiness Divine

Test Transfer

The Lord Bless You And Keep You

The Lord Bless You And Keep You

Test Transfer

The Lord Bless You And Keep You

The Lord Bless You And Keep You

Congratulations, Princess

Congratulations, Princess

90

Congratulations, Princess

God Bless You Graduate

God Bless You Graduate

HONEY

© 1996, PMI

Make Me A Blessing

Make Me A Blessing

Make Me A Blessing

Test Transfer

Angel Of Mercy

Angel Of Mercy

Angel Of Mercy

To Tell The Tooth You're Special

Test Transfer

Love Is Patient

Love Is Patient

Love Is Patient

Test Transfer

May The Sun Always Shine On You

May The Sun Always
Shine On You

SEEDS

Not intended for resale.

© 1996, PMI

Test Transfer

© 1996, PM!

Not intended for resale.

99

The Voice Of Spring

The Voice Of Spring

Test Transfer

Summer's Joy

Summer's Joy

Summer's Joy

Test Transfer

Autumn's Praise

Autumn's Praise

Autumn's Praise

Test Transfer

Winter's Song

Winter's Song

103

Winter's Song

Test Transfer

January Girl

January Girl

104

January Girl

Test Transfer

February Girl

February Girl

February Girl

Test Transfer

March Girl

March Girl

March Girl

April Girl

April Gril

April Girl

Test Transfer

© 1996, PMI
Not intended for resale.

May Girl

May Girl

108

May Girl

June Girl

June Girl

Test Transfer

July Girl

July Girl

July Girl

August Girl

August Girl

August Girl
September Girl

Test Transfer

September Girl

September Girl

September Girl

Test Transfer

© 1996, PMI

October Girl

October Girl

113

October Girl

Test Transfer

November Girl

November Girl

November Girl

Test Transfer

December Girl

December Girl

December Girl

God Is Love, Dear Valentine

God Is Love, Dear Valentine

God Is Love, Dear Valentine

Loving You
Dear Valentine

Loving You
Dear Valentine

Loving You Dear Valentine

117

Loving You
Dear Valentine

Loving You
Dear Valentine

Test Transfer

Easter's On Its Way

Easter's On Its Way

Easter's On Its Way

Test Transfer

Wishing You A Basket Full Of Blessings

Hoppy Easter Friend

Wishing You A Basket Full Of Blessings

Hoppy Easter Friend

Test Transfer

America, You're Beautiful

America, You're Beautiful

America, You're Beautiful

God Bless The USA

God Bless The USA

121

God Bless The USA

Thank You Lord
For Everything

Thank You Lord For Everything

Thank You Lord
For Everything

Test Transfer

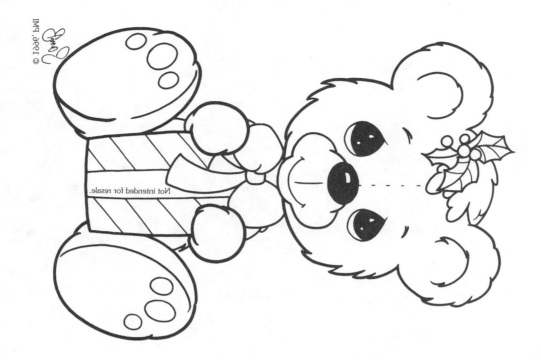

Wishing You A Purr-feet Holiday

Wishing You A Purr-feet Holiday

Wishing You A
Purr-fect Holiday

Test Transfer

Baby's First Christmas

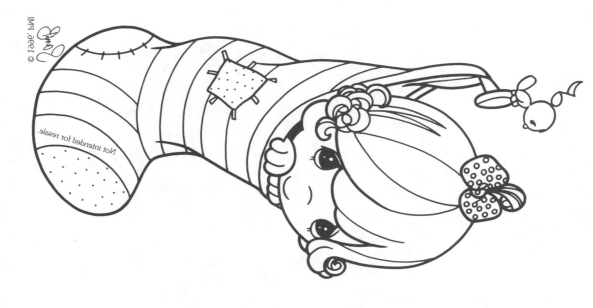

Love Is The Best Gift Of All

Baby's First Christmas
Love Is The Best Gift Of All

124

Test Transfer

I'm Sending You A
White Christmas

I'm Sending You A
White Christmas

Test Transfer

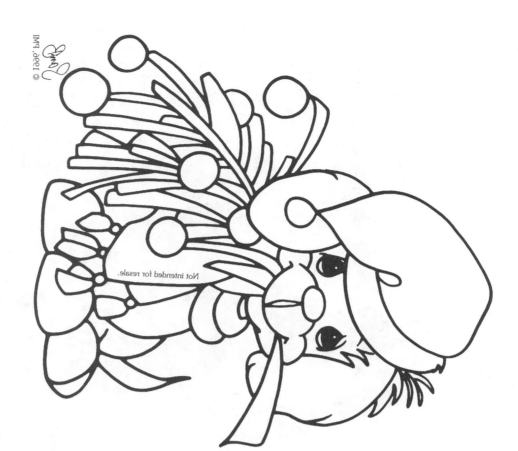

Slow Down And Enjoy The Holidays

Slow Down
And Enjoy The Holidays

Test Transfer

May Your Christmas
Be Delightful

May Your Christmas Be Delightful

We Saw A Star

We Saw A Star

We Saw A Star

Halo, And Merry Christmas

Halo, And Merry Christmas

129

Halo, And Merry Christmas

Peace On Earth

Peace On Earth

Peace On Earth

© 1996, PMI

Bringing God's Blessing To You

Bringing God's Blessing To You

Bringing God's Blessing
To You

Surrounded With Joy

Test Transfer

© 1996, PMI

Not intended for resale.

132

Surrounded With Joy

Surrounded With Joy

I'll Play My Drum for Him

© 1996, PMI

I'll Play My Drum For Him

133

I'll Play
My
Drum
for Him

Let Heaven And Nature Sing

Let Heaven And Nature Sing
Rejoice On Earth

Test Transfer

Rejoice

Rejoice O Earth

Rejoice O Earth

135

Rejoice O Earth

Peace On Earth

© 1996, PMI

Peace On Earth

Peace
On
Earth

Test Transfer

Merry Christmas, Deer

Merry Christmas, Deer

You're As Pretty As A Christmas Tree

You're As Pretty
As A Christmas Tree

Wishing You A Ho Ho Ho

Wishing You A Ho Ho Ho

Ring Those Christmas Bells

Test Transfer

Do Not Open Till Christmas

Do Not Open Till Christmas

Do Not Open till Christmas

May Your World
Be Trimmed With Joy

May Your World Be Trimmed With Joy

142

May Your World
Be Trimmed With Joy

The Wonder Of Christmas

The Wonder Of Christmas

143

The Wonder Of Christmas

Test Transfer

He Is The Star Of The Morning

144

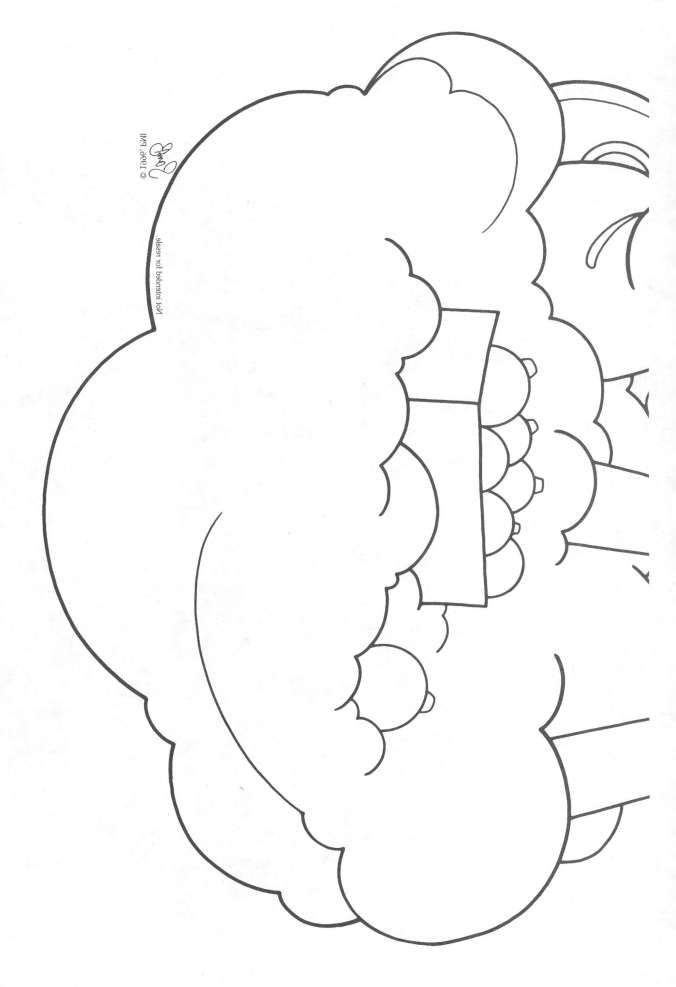

He Is The Star Of The Morning

145

He Is The Star Of The Morning

Test Transfer

Test Transfer

Test Transfer

148

Isn't He Wonderful

Isn't He Wonderful

149

Isn't He Wonderful

Test Transfer

151

Test Transfer

ZAP!

153

0123456789

ABCDEFG
HIJKLMN
OPQRST
UVWXYZ

abcdefg
hijklmn
opqrstu
vwxyz

Alphabets and Numbers — We've included several sizes of alphabets and numbers for you to personalize your garments. There is no right or wrong spacing between letters and words; arrange the letters in a manner pleasing to you. To play with the arrangement of letters and words, first cut out the letters you need. Arrange and rearrange letters as you like on your garment, leaving a space for letters used more than once. When you have decided on placement, tape the letters together on the uninked side with Hot Tape. Place words, ink side down, on garment and transfer.

0123456789

ABCDEF
GHIJKLMN
OPQRST
UVWXYZ

abcdef
ghijklmn
opqrst
uvwxyz

0 1 2 3 4 5 6 7 8 9

a b c d e f g   A B C D E F G

h i j k l m n   H I J K L M N

o p q r s t u   O P Q R S T

v w x y z   U V W X Y Z

Alphabets and Numbers — We've included several sizes of alphabet and numbers for you to personalize your garments. There is no right or wrong spacing between letters and words. To play with the arrangement of letters and words, first cut out the letters you need. Arrange and rearrange letters as you like on your garment, leaving a space of letters used more than once. When you have decided on placement, iron the letters face down on the unlined side with light tape. Place words inside down for garment and trace.

0 1 2 3 4 5 6 7 8 9

a b c d e f   A B C D E F

g h i j k l m n   G H I J K L M N

o p q r s t u   O P Q R S T

v w x y z   U V W X Y Z

ABCDEFGHIJ
KLMNOPQRS
TUVWXYZ

0123456789

abcdefghij
klmnopqrs
tuvwxyz

0123456789

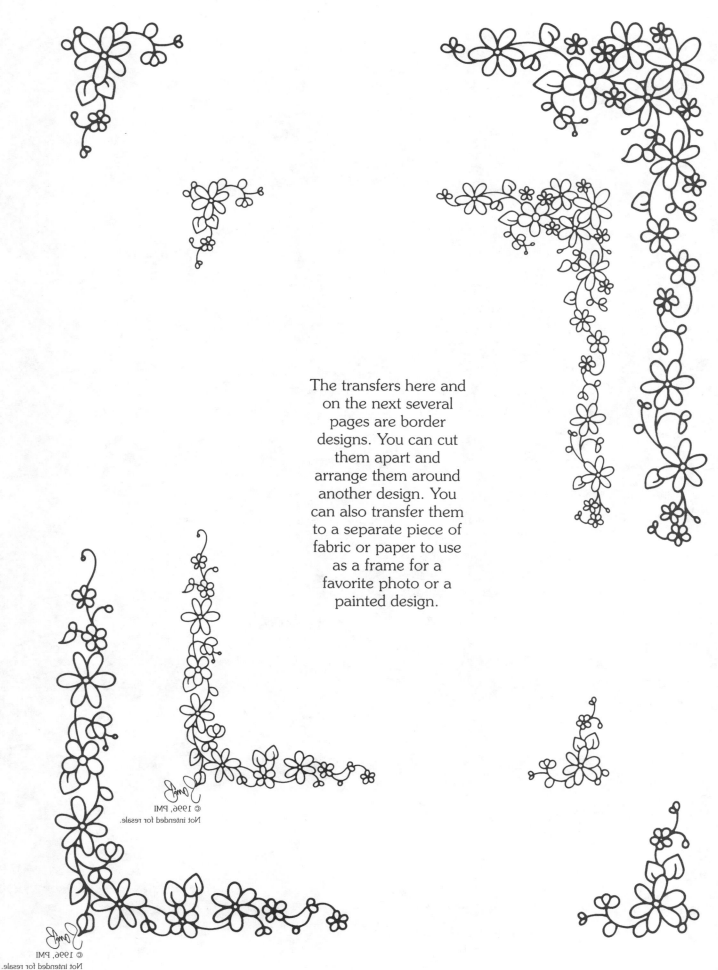

The transfers here and on the next several pages are border designs. You can cut them apart and arrange them around another design. You can also transfer them to a separate piece of fabric or paper to use as a frame for a favorite photo or a painted design.

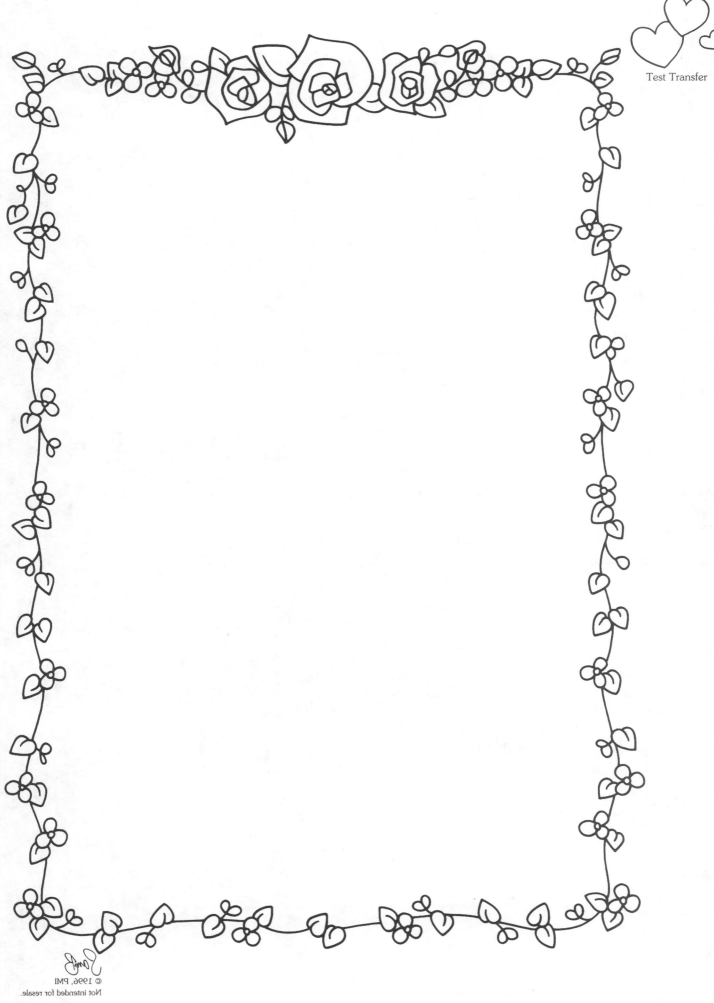

Test Transfer

Test Transfer

Test Transfer

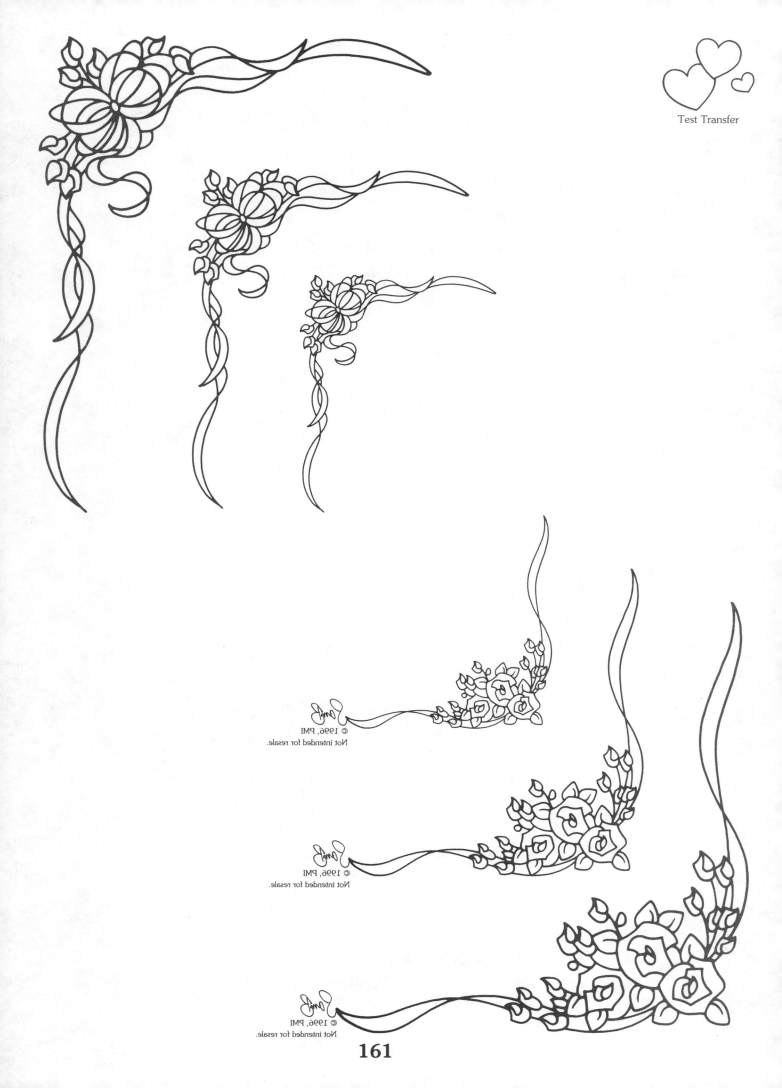

Test Transfer

Test Transfer

Test Transfer

163

Test Transfer

Test Transfer

167

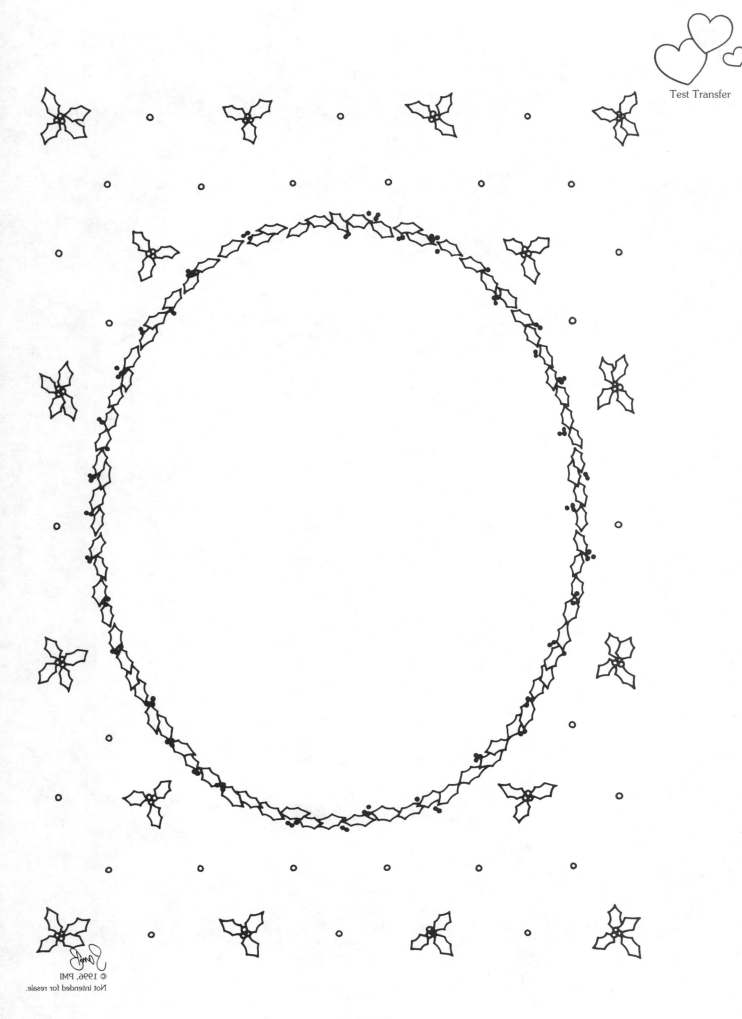

Test Transfer

Test Transfer